BATS

by Lily Wood

SCHOLASTIC INC.

New York   Toronto   London   Sydney
Auckland   Mexico City   New Delhi!   Hong Kong

SCHOLASTIC READER • LEVEL 1
50–250 WORDS

P9-DGG-039

This edition first printing, September 2010

Printed in the U.S.A.   40

10 9 8 7 6 5 4 3 2 1   10 11 12 13 14/0

Lexile is a registered trademark of MetaMetrics, Inc.

ISBN 978-0-545-23754-3

Robert & Linda Mitchell; p. 29: © Theo Allofs/Getty Images; p. 30: © Phil Date/iStockphoto.
Rennteester Inc./The Image Bank/Getty Images; pp. 26–27: © John Downer/ Getty Images; p. 28: ©
pp. 20–21: © Nick Upton/Nature Picture Library; pp. 22–23: © Johner Images/Alamy; pp. 24–25: © Co
Four Oaks/ Shutterstock; pp. 16–17: © Graeme Knox/ Shutterstock; p. 18: © John Panelo/Shutterstock;
lin D. Tuttle/BCI; p. 11: © Susan Flashman/Shutterstock; p. 13: © WILDLIFE GmbH/Alamy, p. 15: ©
History Unit; p. 6: © Rick & Nora Bowers/Alamy, p. 7: © Dietmar Nill/ Minden Pictures; pp. 8–9: © Mer-
p. 2, p. 12: Merlin D. Tuttle/BCI; p. 3: © Ra'id Khalil/ Shutterstock; pp. 4–5: © Dietmar Nill/BBC Natural
Front cover, p. 1: © Ingo Arndt/Minden Pictures; (inset): © Dietmar Nill/ Minden Pictures; back cover.

Photo Credits

Bats are interesting animals. There are more than 1,000 types of bats. Bats live all over the world.

Bats live in caves. Some bats can be found inside trees.

Other bats live in attics. Sometimes bats can even be seen under bridges.

Bats sleep upside down. Bats have claws that cling to trees and cave walls.

Bats fly. But bats are not birds.
Birds have feathers. Bats do not.
Bats have fur.

Bats are **mammals**. Bats are the only mammals that fly.

Some bats live in small families. Other bats live in large groups. Large or small, these groups are called **colonies**.

Each year a mother bat usually has one **pup**. A pup is a baby bat.

The mother bat needs to find food for her pup. While the mother bat hunts for food, the pup stays home.

Most bats eat bugs or fruit.
Some bats drink the sweet
juice inside flowers.

Bats help farmers. Many catch bugs that eat farmers' crops.

Like bees, some bats carry pollen from plant to plant when they rub against them. This helps plants make seeds.

Bats use sound to find their way at night. The sound comes back to the bat's ears as an echo. This is called **echolocation**.

Vampire bats bite cows and birds. They drink a tiny bit of blood for food.

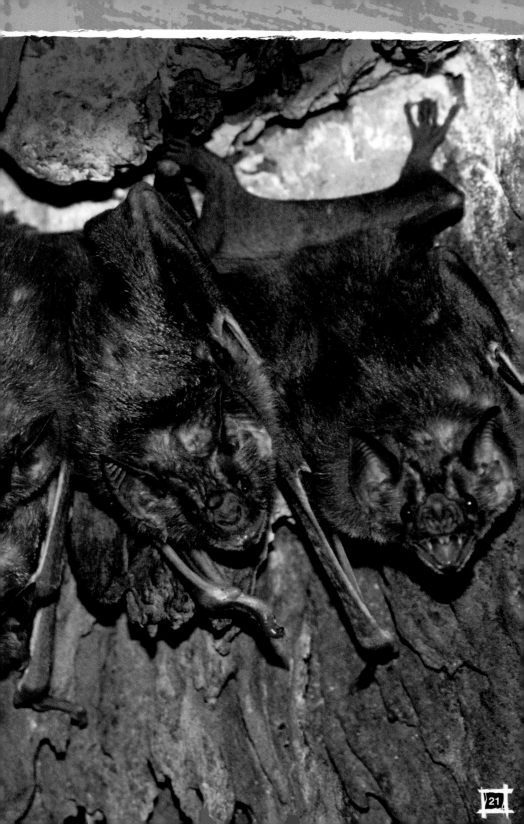

Long-eared bats fly during the night. They use echolocation to find food when they are hungry.

They eat moths, spiders, and other insects.

In winter some bats **migrate.**

These bats travel to warmer places for the winter.

Other bats **hibernate**. They spend th
winter in a cave, a building, or a tree

When a bat hibernates, its heartbeat and breathing slow down.

Today it is hard for bats to find homes. Many trees have been cut down.

It is important for people to protect bats and their homes so they do not become extinct.

Bats come in all shapes and sizes. No matter where they live, bats are interesting animals.

GLOSSARY

Colonies – groups of animals, such as bats, that live together in the same place

Echolocation (ek-oh-loh-**kay**-shuhn) – to find (locate) objects by sending out sounds, then listening to the sound that bounces back (the echo)

Hibernate (**hye**-bur-nate) – to enter a sleeplike state in winter

Mammals – animals that feed milk to their babies

Migrate (**mye**-grate) – to take a seasonal journey from one place to another

Pup – a baby bat